WILD DORSET

Following pages
Mitchell's Ten Acres, one of the herb-rich hay meadows on
the ancient field system at Kingcombe Meadows.

WILD DORSET
The Year in Photographs

Colin Varndell

THE DOVECOTE PRESS

For Susy, Holly and Emily

Mosses are primitive plants and actively grow during the cool, moist
winter months. In March, they sprout spore capsules, which
eventually wither after the spores are released.

First published in 2004 by The Dovecote Press Ltd
Stanbridge, Wimborne Minster, Dorset BH21 4JD

ISBN 1 904349 35 8

Text and photographs © Colin Varndell 2004

Colin Varndell has asserted his rights under the Copyright, Designs
and Patent Act 1988 to be identified as author of this work

Designed by The Dovecote Press
Printed and bound in Singapore

All papers used by The Dovecote Press are natural, recyclable products
made from wood grown in sustainable, well-managed forests

A CIP catalogue record for this book is available
from the British Library

CONTENTS

INTRODUCTION

Sitting beneath an old hawthorn on the bank of the River Asker, near Bradpole, I watched a pair of dippers collecting aquatic insects to feed their hungry nestlings. In the distance, above the sound of the water, I heard a faint but sharp whistle. The noise was repeated, growing gradually closer and becoming a high-pitched, piercing note. It was the call of a male kingfisher, which I caught sight of as it flew low over the river and came to rest on an old wooden fence post on the opposite bank. The bird stared fiercely into the water, repeatedly bobbing its head. It was about 5 metres from me, and I sat motionless as I watched. 'Plop!' In a flash the

kingfisher was back on its perch, this time with a wriggling minnow in its beak. It gripped the minnow by the tail and repeatedly bashed it against the fence post before swallowing it headfirst. Almost immediately, a second kingfisher came hurtling up the river. As it passed, the male leapt from the post and took chase. The two birds disappeared from view but I could hear their excited, piping calls for some time.

It was April 1976, and I remember an overwhelming feeling of the need to share this wonderful experience with others. The next day I bought a 35mm camera and a telephoto lens. In the afternoon, I sat on the riverbank hoping the kingfishers would perform for me again. Of course they didn't, but I was smitten, and from that day I spent all of my spare time in pursuit of wildlife pictures.

To begin with I concentrated on photographing birds, as I had a special interest in bird behaviour. Later, I expanded my interest to encompass mammals, plants and insects, eventually specialising in all aspects of nature in Dorset, including landscape and weather. I have photographed over 500 species of plant, 200 birds, most of the county's butterflies and dragonflies and now work with a collection of around 160,000 images.

The notion of a nature photographer wandering around the countryside shooting pictures of wild animals and birds as they present themselves could not be further from the truth. Each subject requires reconnaissance, planning, preparation, the use of specialist equipment and – more often than not – endless patience.

For example, I once sat in my cramped hide for 6 hour sessions on 8 consecutive days to get one photograph of a running female roe deer. Early on, together with the help of friends, I built a scaffold hide 70 feet up in the woodland canopy to photograph buzzards at the nest. When it was finished, I spent the longest day in June sitting in the treetops from dawn until dusk, but didn't take a single photograph!

Some subjects are stalked in the open, like this reed warbler, which I photographed at Radipole in May. It is vital to remain perfectly still, and only move forward when the subject looks away.

The boredom of waiting for endless hours for something which may not even happen is not easy to cope with. I am not naturally a patient man, and I've had to train myself to remain motionless and alert for hour after hour. Unfortunately, you can't relax and read a book, as most animals and birds are essentially silent. I remember sitting in my hide on the edge of the Fleet lagoon and had that feeling that something was watching me. I slowly turned to see a heron standing about 5 feet from my hide. On another occasion, I had set up an open-topped hide near a bathing pool in woodland. A male sparrowhawk perched on one of the hide poles for nearly an hour during which time I struggled to remain still. The end result though can be hugely rewarding, and one instantly forgets the tedium and the inordinate amount of time it took.

I enjoy every aspect of my work, but that is not to say that

I spent eight long afternoons in a cramped hide for this one photograph of a running roe deer.

it is easy. There are many difficulties and discomforts, the midges and horseflies; the wasps which are attracted to my camouflage material; backache, knee-ache and the penetrating cold. Who in their right mind would choose to sit outside in a deck chair for several hours in January? But to get winter wildlife pictures, that's what it takes.

When I set out to photograph wild mammals I carry a bag containing food and drink, a portable hide; hide frame; seat; tripod; two cameras and at least two lenses - one of which is a 500mm. Often this heavy kit has to be carried long distances over difficult terrain which nearly always seems to be uphill!

In 1989, I had the opportunity to turn what was then my

The heron waits with endless patience for signs of movement in the water. I have spent many hours waiting in hides for a heron to strike so as to photograph it in the act of catching a fish.

hobby into a full time career. Since then I have divided my working week between writing, taking new photographs and running a picture library business.

Keeping pace with the seasons is probably the most difficult aspect of this work. For instance, although we see bluebells for several weeks in spring, they are only at their best for a couple of days, and they have to be photographed then. The weeks go by quickly and bring changes with them throughout the year. I have kept field notebooks for 30 years and I constantly refer to them when planning a season of photography. I also keep a mental collection of images I hope to capture in my mind. Some of these ideas come to fruition quickly, others can take years before I encounter in reality what had been a vague conception in my thoughts.

I have never felt a desire to go abroad for pictures. It is the wildlife that surrounds us here in Dorset which fascinates me. The aim of this book is to document both Dorset's landscape and its natural history throughout the course of a year. Subtle changes continuously occur in the countryside, in response to weather conditions and merging seasons. When the spring daffodils are at their best we marvel at their vivid trumpets, but within days they fade to dull green seedpods with tissue paper foliage. On other occasions, we are blessed with spring blossom; the butterflies of summer; the warm colours of autumn and the frosts of winter. Think of this book as a series of snapshots into the wild lands of Dorset, where deer run, buzzards soar and dragonflies meander along quiet streams.

I hope this book helps the reader in some small way to gain a greater insight into the varied richness that Dorset's natural history has to offer. As the changes in the countryside wax and wane, so the story unfolds of the annual cycles of the wildlife and landscape of this wonderful county in which I am privileged to live and photograph.

COLIN VARNDELL
Netherbury, Dorset
OCTOBER 2004

JANUARY

JANUARY

ON A BLEAK January morning it is difficult to imagine a frozen Dorset heath bursting into life with literally millions of insects in just a few months time. Frosted bracken fronds crunch underfoot; ghostly vapours emanate from the damp bogs. The grasp of winter penetrates the earth, and the only sound reminiscent of summer is the buzzing call of a Dartford warbler as it flits amongst the gorse in a tireless search for food.

Dartford warblers are small and stubborn. Their determination to remain in England through the bitterly cold winters of the 1960s reduced their numbers to no more than ten pairs, most of them in Dorset. They are insect-eaters, and thus are especially vulnerable during persistent, freezing conditions when their food supply is hidden beneath a carpet of snow or hard frost. Recent relatively mild winters have brought a marked improvement in their fortunes, and Dorset's Dartford warbler population is now much healthier. As well as on its characteristic home of lowland heath, it can now be heard amidst stands of gorse or stunted blackthorn.

January is usually the coldest month, marking the mid point of Dorset's winter. Short days make life difficult for resident wild animals and birds, with limited daylight to forage and prolonged hours of darkness. These unfavourable odds are compounded by the prospect of extreme weather setting in without warning. Unremitting periods of severe cold can spell disaster for much of the county's wildlife. Small animals need to feed frequently in order to maintain their energy levels. Shrews, for example, cannot survive for more than about two hours without food, and many of the smaller birds require daily intakes of nourishment equal to their own bodyweight.

But January can bring beauty as well as peril. Freshly fallen snow has a magical effect on the landscape, decorating every hedgerow and tree, transforming the hills and valleys into an enchanted winter wonderland. Arguably, winter's greatest gift is hoarfrost, which in clear, sub-zero conditions is formed as contrasting temperatures of day and night produce condensation, which freezes to twigs as wafer-thin blades of white ice.

The bare skeletons of deciduous trees reveal an underlying beauty when decorated with hoarfrost, or silhouetted against the afterglow of a January sunset. Near Badbury Rings, a

PREVIOUS PAGE Almost every copse and wood throughout Dorset will have a resident pair of tawny owls. These strictly nocturnal birds become active during January when pairing takes place and the proposed nest site is established.

LEFT Insects spend winter in various forms. These herald moths were discovered hibernating as adults under a bench in a garden shed.

ABOVE Winter heliotrope is typically found on shady damp banks in the west of the county. It is closely related to the more common butterbur and is in flower during January, but the leaves continue to grow throughout the spring and summer.

RIGHT Hoarfrost often occurs in river valleys like the Frome and Piddle where moisture rising from the water surface forms freezing fog to decorate bushes and trees with ice crystals.

magnificent avenue of elderly beeches stand like a regiment of undressed sentries. Sadly, these majestic trees are now well past their prime and gaps are begnning to appear in their ranks. Happily, a replacement avenue has been planted as a memorial to PC Yvonne Fletcher, who was gunned down outside the Libyan Embassy in 1984.

Even in midwinter, not all plant life remains dormant; mosses and lichens prefer its moister conditions to sprout lush new growth; some species of fungi continue to produce fruiting bodies; buds of trees are already swelling and catkins start to expand. Winter heliotrope, a relative of the more commonly known butterbur, flowers on damp, shady banks, and the progress of developing snowdrops is noticeable as buds swell and the first white petals appear.

These early flowers are pollinated by hardy insects, and if the weather is mild may even be visited by bumblebees. But the majority of insects remain in hiding in egg or pupae form, or as hibernating adults, snugly nestled into crevices and hollows, or tucked away behind tree bark.

ABOVE Frost crystals decorate the patterned fronds of dead bracken.

BELOW The mole is designed for rapid digging and tunnelling. It's front paws have broad, outward angled palms, with strong claws which serve as efficient picks.

While most wild creatures concentrate on survival, some mammals are already preparing for busier times ahead. Freshly excavated soil at badger earths is evidence that preparations for nursery accommodation are under way. Badgers either dig fresh chambers each year, or renovate old ones in which to raise their young. This method of spring-cleaning helps to prevent a build-up of parasites from season to season.

As badgers prepare for the birth of their young, foxes are at a much earlier stage of their annual breeding cycle. The fox mating season typically lasts from mid-December until late January, and the unearthly sound of foxes calling after dark is common throughout the county. The husky mating cry of the vixen sounds more like a distress call than an alluring one, as she calls to proclaim her desire to mate.

An irrepressible yearning to reproduce stirs in other wild creatures too. The remarkable sound of massed croaking bullfrogs is only heard for a few nights at this time of year. Frogs hibernate during winter, but on mild, damp nights they move toward their breeding ponds. Frogs can spawn as early as the first week in January, and will certainly lay eggs before

ABOVE Freezing temperatures, preceding a weather front from the north or east can bring significant falls of snow, as in this picture of North Poorton, with the hills of Lewesdon and Pilsdon beyond.

RIGHT The frog mating season is partly dependent upon weather conditions, but in Dorset, January is the month when mating usually starts to takes place.

the end of the month if weather conditions are favourable. In the comparative safety of darkness, bullfrogs emit their guttural, chirring songs to entice females to join them. A female will lay up to 2,000 eggs in one night, and usually, mating activity at any given site will only last for a few days. The accompanying din acts as a magnet for predators. Foxes and herons take both frogs and spawn, and buzzards have been recorded swooping down to snatch frogs from West Dorset ponds.

Tawny owls become more vocal after dark as they rekindle their pair bonds in readiness for breeding. The tawny is Dorset's commonest owl, and almost every wood and copse in the county has a resident pair. The haunting 'Who-oo-oo-oo' call is given by the male to assert his territorial ownership – the female replies with a penetrating, high-pitched 'kee-wick'.

Large numbers of geese and ducks congregate on the Fleet lagoon, and Poole Harbour is home to flocks of over-wintering waders. At low tide, these birds feed in the shallow water or by probing the mudflats with their specialised bills. Radipole Lake's varied habitats make it particularly attractive to birds. Gulls, cormorants and grebes occupy the open water along with rafts of tufted duck and shoveller. The once rare little egret stalks fish in sheltered pools. The reed beds are home to reed bunting and Cetti's warbler, whilst the handsome bearded tit can often be seen feeding on reed seed heads. The RSPB reserve at Lodmoor also supports many over-wintering birds. At high tide, waders and wildfowl fly in to rest within the relative safety of the reserve. Flocks of lapwing and golden plover are usually present throughout January, and a sudden cold snap might tempt the elusive water rail to venture out from the reeds in search of food.

Typically at this time of year, many birds form flocks,

ABOVE The common shrew is one of Dorset's smallest mammals. It lives on a diet of insects, worms and snails, and is unable to survive for more than two hours without food. Like the mole, the shrew has short, soft, velvety fur to enable it to move through soil without getting dirty.

partly because it increases the chance of finding food, partly to provide better protection against predators. A huge flock of starlings traditionally perform coordinated flight displays over reedbeds at West Bexington on January afternoons. Along hedgerows, and in woods and gardens, mixed parties of tits forage for insects. Beech mast attracts flocks of chaffinches, greenfinches and occasionally bramblings. Linnets and yellowhammers congregate on arable fields to scavenge for leftovers from the autumn harvest.

Despite the cold and the struggle for survival, some birds are already anticipating spring. Woodpeckers and robins form pairs in preparation for breeding, and herons will have put the final touches to their nests and begun to lay eggs by the end of the month.

As January fades, birds and animals begin to display a certain restlessness. The songs of songthrush, robin and wren increase in both frequency and volume, as if they seem to know that winter's back is almost broken.

ABOVE The bearded tit is found in a few of Dorset's coastal reedbeds, as here at Radipole Lake.

BELOW In some years, when the Scandinavian rowan crop is poor, huge numbers of waxwings migrate to Britain. Their need for berries in late winter, together with the sheer pressure of numbers, brought this one to a housing estate in Wareham, where it was feeding on cotoneaster and pyracantha berries.

BELOW A blue tit about to land on a bird-feeder. The bird fans its tail to create maximum air resistance in order to slow itself down.

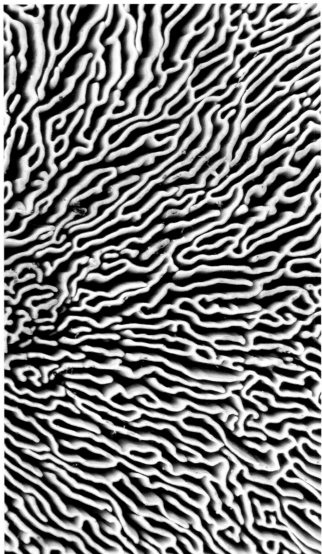

ABOVE The maze-gill (*daedalea quercina*) fungus is so-called because of the gills on the underside which resemble a maze. This fungus is restricted to decaying oak wood in Dorset and may be found on fallen branches or dead oak stumps.

LEFT The chalk cliffs of Swyre Head and Bat's Head photographed from Durdle Door in the low, winter sunlight of a January day.

FEBRUARY

FEBRUARY

SOMETIMES it seems as if February always arrives on a cold, dank morning. It may be the shortest month, but often feels like the longest. Yet in reality February brings mixed blessings. With barely a by-your-leave, a run of bleak midwinter days can be followed by others bearing the promise of spring. Regardless of the weather, changes take place in the countryside, which at first are almost imperceptible, though by the end of the month wildlife activity will have gathered momentum.

During February, the huge flock of avocets which has gathered on the lagoon at Brownsea Island reaches its peak.

Over the past few years their numbers have grown to well over 1,000, and they now form one of the largest flocks of avocets to be seen in Britain. These elegant waders feed in the

PREVIOUS PAGE Brown hares are easy to see at this time of year before the crops grow. Although hare 'boxing' is associated with late winter, such behaviour can be seen at any time of year.

BELOW The over-wintering flock of avocets in Poole Harbour must be one of the most spectacular wildlife sights in Dorset, if not in the wider country. Here they are shown exploding into the air together with a flock of black-tailed godwits.

shallows of the lagoon, sweeping their upturned bills from side to side to capture small invertebrates from the water's surface. Occasionally they erupt in synchronised flight, black wing markings flashing in unison, their melodious calls echoing out over Poole Harbour to provide a welcome contrast to the loud honk of Brent geese.

Elsewhere along the coast, the fulmar petrel soars over the sea in typical stiff-winged attitude before plunging towards the cliff where at the last split second it winnows to free-fall away from the rock face. In late winter, fulmars begin to

ABOVE Early morning mist floats between the hills in this tranquil scene at Hincknowle. Two gamekeepers can be seen walking with their dogs at the bottom of the photograph.

occupy their precarious nest sites on rock ledges. As they jostle for position, quarrelling occurs over prime locations, giving rise to an extraordinary noise resembling cackling laughter.

Although February might seem a barren month for plant life, the observant will soon spot spring's first stirrings. Hazel

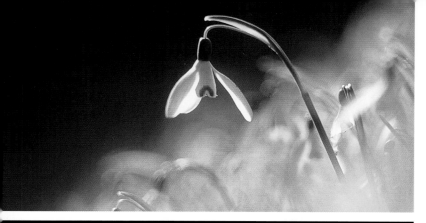

UPPER LEFT The snowdrop is not a native wild flower to Dorset. It was probably introduced from Turkey and is now firmly established as a naturalised wild flower.

ABOVE Many woodland wild flowers have produced abundant foliage by now. These herb Robert leaves are edged with frost crystals.

LEFT Hazel catkins are the male flowers, which produce pollen during February and March to pollinate the tiny female blooms, which will become the hazelnuts of autumn.

catkins decorate Dorset's hedgerows and copses, dangling in the breeze to pollinate the tiny, insignificant female flowers, which will become the hazelnuts of autumn. On banks and in woods the delicate appearance of snowdrops belie their robust, rugged nature. Wild snowdrops are in full flower and at their prime by mid-February, and despite their apparent daintiness, they are hardier flowers than most. In wooded valleys – like those at Mapperton and Burcombe – their drooping white blooms are so dense they give the impression of a dusting of snow. In woodland, mosses grow bright new fronds to replace the dull brown relics of winter, and the first bluebell leaves push up through the leaf litter. Wild daffodil buds begin to show in sheltered pockets, and roadside banks are flecked with early primroses.

One of the most characteristic sounds of February is the drumming of great spotted woodpeckers. These handsome

ABOVE The scarlet elf cup fungus is usually evident at snowdrop time. It is especially plentiful in damp areas of light woodland where it grows on mossy stumps and dead wood.

BELOW The bright green shoots of an emerging crop of winter wheat with the village of Stour Provost in the distance.

birds rapidly bang their beaks on hollow boughs to advertise their territories. Although both sexes can 'drum', it is usually the male that undertakes this annual task, at an extraordinary eighteen 'hits' per second. It has been calculated that each 'hit' is the equivalent of a car slamming into a brick wall at 40 miles an hour. The woodpecker's brain floats in a cushion of tissue to lessen the impact and prevent damage.

Not all birds lay claim to their territories so forcefully. Most birds use song, and at dawn there is already a murmuring prelude of what is to come. Male birds sing to establish nesting territories and attract potential mates. Some species, like robin, songthrush and wren, do so during the winter to maintain their feeding territories, but now their song becomes an eager invitation for females to join them. Other birds, though gregarious throughout winter, become less tolerant of their neighbours as the beginning of the breeding season awakes an instinct for pairing up with potential mates. Starling flocks disperse as individual birds spring clean and prepare their nests. Parties of long tailed tits divide into pairs and rarely visit bird tables in gangs.

Members of the crow family are at the early stages of nest building. At rookeries, squabbling frequently breaks out as

rogue individuals rob sticks from neighbouring nests. Rooks are sociable, returning year after year to their treetop rookeries - though there is little truth in the old country saying that if rooks build high then the weather will be fine in the months ahead. The truth is that sudden cold snaps are common in February, posing a real threat to those like the heron and raven, which already are incubating eggs.

For other birds the main threat lies in the lack of food. Siskin and goldfinch typically feed on alder seeds in winter, but by February supplies are exhausted, forcing them to set aside their natural shyness and visit garden bird tables. Flocks of redwing and fieldfare passing through Dorset as they migrate eastward have even slenderer pickings if it suddenly turns cold. In mild weather, they forage on farmland and hedgerow fruits, but if temperatures plummet their only option is turning over woodland leaf litter in search of beetles and grubs.

Toads arrive at ponds to spawn towards the end of the month, entwining their necklace-like strands of black eggs around submerged vegetation. Toads do not call to attract mates in the same way as frogs do, but generally remain silent during mating. Their occasional squeaks are given by males warning other amorous individuals to get off their backs. A male toad in a sexual frenzy will grasp anything resembling a potential mate – even another male!

Wild mammals also respond to the increasing hours of daylight, and many of them will have started their breeding cycles by now. Although bats, hedgehogs and dormice remain in hibernation for a while yet, badgers and grey squirrels both give birth during February. Deep underground, in the warmth and safety of specially prepared nursery chambers, blind and naked badger cubs are born. The usual litter size is two or three, and they remain below ground until they are between 6 and 8 weeks old. Grey squirrels give birth in large, stick nests, or dreys. The usual number of young is three and they too are born naked and blind and are weaned within three months.

Female foxes are now heavily pregnant and there is noticeable frisky behaviour in rabbit communities. On the chalk downlands and arable fields in the north of the county, Jack hares may be seen in groups, eager to mate with females as they come into season.

RIGHT The epitome of a sleepy West Dorset village – Cattistock, before dawn on a frosty February morning.

ABOVE The harbour at Lyme Regis is home to both boats and birds. On a typical February day at low tide, rock pipits, pied wagtails and even black redstarts might be seen here.

Fallow deer congregate in mixed herds of both sexes at this time, the bucks retaining their previous year's antlers. The fallow is native to southern Europe and is thought to have been first introduced to Britain by the Normans. The herds in the woodland around Powerstock and Hooke are regarded as descendants of some of the earliest introductions. It is not unusual to see groups of 40-50 of these dark coated deer grazing the farmland below Eggardon Hill in daytime.

If conditions are mild towards the end of February, insects will start to venture out to visit catkins and the early spring flowers. Honeybees become active and even those butterflies which have spent winter at the adult stage, may make their initial sorties on the wing. By the end of the month blackbirds deliver their flutey songs at dawn and dusk, an indication that winter is almost over.

ABOVE This field vole is eating the succulent shoots of golden saxifrage, a woodland flower which thrives in boggy habitats at this time of year.

RIGHT Yellowhammers readily visit bird feeders at this time of year as there is very little natural seed available for them in the countryside.

In late winter, dunnocks engage in 'wing flicking' which forms part
of their prenuptial display. Both sexes do this as males constantly
pursue females.

MARCH

MARCH

The beginning of spring is symbolised by lengthening days and rising temperatures, accelerating the changes in the countryside. Wild weather with boisterous south-westerly winds, typical of March, can easily bring down old trees and whip the sea into a raging assault on the Dorset coast. Above the wind's roar can be heard the melancholy song of the mistlethrush, hence its nickname 'stormcock'.

PREVIOUS PAGE The common primrose is one of the true delights of March in Dorset. It likes to flower on the sunny banks of country lanes and along the edges of woodland in dappled light.

BELOW Thin evening sun lights up a storm at Burton Bradstock.

The native daffodils of Powerstock Common, Burcombe Valley and the Marshwood Vale bloom early. Their dainty, short-lived trumpets are spent before the main crop of tawdry, cultivated varieties garnish town parks and village gardens. The primrose on the other hand has a long flowering season, preferring sunny banks on which to display its creamy yellow flowers. In Dorset, primroses often hybridise with cowslips to produce false oxlip plants. Although these unusual crossbreeds are perennial, they seldom have a long lifespan and may not reappear the following spring.

The most significant change in the county's birdlife this month is the sudden departure of wildfowl. This migration usually passes unnoticed, and often one is not aware of it until

The chiff-chaff is the first of the summer visitors to take up residence in woods and gardens.

A male Dartford warbler sings from a gorse bush on Winfrith Heath to proclaim his breeding territory.

long after the birds are gone. Instead, our attention is drawn to the arrival of the first early summer visitors, heralded by the monotonous song of the chiff-chaff. Another early migrant to appear is the wheatear, landing first at Portland, where it was once served up as a delicacy, then moving on to the chalk downlands of north Dorset, where the male celebrates surviving its long flight from Africa with a wonderful dancing courtship display. Typically, this alert, white-rumped bird perches on fence posts on the steep downs, from where it chases and darts after early insects.

On arable farmland in the north and east of the county, the flirtatious courtship of the lapwing is played out in an elaborate tumbling flight display. While this is the beginning of the breeding season for most birds, some are already committed to their nests. Mallard ducks sit tight in thick vegetation incubating their first clutch of eggs. Like most species of female duck, the mallard has evolved drab, mottled plumage, providing the necessary camouflage at this critical time. Both mallard and her eggs have many potential enemies.

A roving fox would eagerly devour a dozen or so eggs, and the capture of an adult duck would be a nutritious prize for hungry cubs. Fox cubs are developing fast, and as they become weaned the need for an ample supply of fresh meat increases.

The dipper is a bird of fast flowing rivers and streams, feeding on aquatic invertebrates such as water-boatmen and dragonfly nymphs. This white-bibbed bird is one of the delights of West Dorset rivers, such as the Brit and Asker, where it nests under bridges or behind overhanging vegetation on walls.

Nuthatches appropriate redundant woodpecker nests and plaster mud around the entrance to reduce the hole size, thus denying access to would-be predators, including woodpeckers! Blackbirds are also early nesters, and are capable of rearing up to five broods of young in one season. By mid-March the first podgy, speckled young blackbirds appear in gardens. They are fed mainly by the adult male, as the female is too busy with her next clutch of eggs.

Buzzards congregate overhead, wheeling on the thermals and uttering their pathetic mewing cries as they establish their breeding order. The buzzard is a lazy hunter, and can often be seen wandering about in fields scavenging for earthworms or beetles. In early spring though, an abundance of unwary young rabbits provides an easy source of food, on which it swoops mercilessly. Rabbits quickly learn caution. Stoats and foxes regularly enter their warrens, and the sharp-eyed tawny owl is quick to spot a young rabbit on open ground.

Even though the weather becomes noticeably warmer during March, many of the seed eating birds still struggle to survive. Yellowhammers, greenfinches and collared doves eagerly visit garden bird tables. Others find nutrition in early fruits. Ripening ivy berries are a favourite of blackbirds and woodpigeons, who regurgitate the indigestible pips. Bullfinches enthusiastically nip off the buds of hawthorn, forsythia and apple trees, earning themselves an unpopular reputation amongst fruit growers.

But even the bullfinches can't halt the seasonal cycle. Hesitantly at first, but in ever greater number, buds swell and break as native trees and shrubs begin a new season of growth. Although the main flush of spring foliage is still some weeks away, hawthorn, sycamore, elder and silver birch all break into leaf during March.

A steady succession of wild flowers follows suit. Pink purslane, an uncommon annual in Britain, has its national stronghold in West Dorset and Devon, occurring in damp, open woodland. Greater stitchwort opens its delicate white flowers amongst thick clumps of budding bluebells, and the white petals of the wood anemone (or Easter flower as it is locally known) can be seen on sunny woodland banks. Persian speedwell, periwinkle and ground ivy are all considered weeds in gardens, but in the wild they provide

UPPER LEFT Bramblings over-winter in Dorset and may turn up at garden bird feeders in March. This male is changing from dull winter plumage into his rich breeding colours.

CENTRE LEFT The haunting calls of whimbrel echo along the Fleet Lagoon as they pass through on their way to summer breeding grounds.

LEFT The flamboyant great crested grebes at Radipole Lake engage in elaborate courtship displays during early March.

ABOVE Stormy weather can be typical in March. This view from Eggardon Hill is bathed in sharp, afternoon sunlight, while the next heavy rain cloud approaches menacingly from the west.

RIGHT The wood anemone has many local names. In West Dorset it is known as the Easter flower as its blooms often coincide with Eastertide.

important nectar sources for insects. The tiny muscatel, with its five green clock faces, blooms in Dorset's mature hedgerows and is considered to be indicative of ancient woodland.

Horsetails produces their translucent spore cones long before their foliage is visible, and the ghostlike flowers of the parasitic toothwort appear at the base of hazel clumps. Woodland ferns begin to unfurl and dog's mercury and arum lily (known locally in West Dorset as 'parsons in their pulpits') begin to show amongst wooded undergrowth. Along

ABOVE Kimmeridge Bay is a marine nature reserve and due to its proximity of being halfway along the English Channel, supports several species of marine life that are at or near their normal distribution limits.

LEFT The small tortoiseshell spends winter hibernating in adult form. On warm days during March they emerge to mate and lay eggs.

the coast, erect stands of celery-like alexanders are recognizable by their green florets of umbillifer blooms. This native wild flower thrives when occasionally drenched by salt spray from the sea, and seldom flourishes far inland. Its early blooms offer a nectar supply for insects, who in turn provide a welcome meal for migrating birds reaching landfall. But of all Dorset's wild flowers in March, the greatest impact is made by the lowly gorse, its bright yellow flowers adding a

splash of colour to much of the county.

On fine days, adders appear above ground to bask in the warm spring sunshine. They coil drowsily on the same stone or anthill, staying close to their hibernation holes and retreating below ground as soon as the weather worsens.

The brimstone butterfly also takes advantage of the warmth. After a winter spent hiding in evergreen foliage, it now emerges to dance erratically along the lanes and hedges as a mesmerising blur of sulphur yellow. Small tortoiseshell and peacock butterflies also venture onto the wing in mild conditions. Hoverflies pollinate the early spring flora, and the bee fly hovers over primrose plants, dipping its long proboscis deep into the flowers. Not all insects are so welcome. All over Dorset, queen wasps venture from their hiding places, anxious to begin construction work on new paper nests.

LEFT The flowerless horsetail is a relative of the coal forest trees, which grew 250 million years ago. During March, the pinkish-brown spore stems appear. These are devoid of any green colouring and die back once the spores are shed.

BELOW Blackthorn is the first of our native trees to blossom. Its delicate white flowers break into bloom along the hedgerows throughout March.

ABOVE During March, adders bask on sunny afternoons near their hibernating holes.

BELOW Despite its national rarity, the crested newt is quite common during March in some of the wild ponds of West Dorset.

APRIL

APRIL

PRIL STARTS with lanes peppered yellow with a vibrant mix of cowslip, primrose, celandine and yellow archangel. Bright yellow bracts of wood spurge appear in copses, and goat willow trees bear downy, golden catkins. The sense of expectation that began in March finally becomes a reality as the Dorset countryside bursts into new life. The incredible sounds and smells of April are generated by the resurgence of plants and animals at the pinnacle of their life cycles. Whilst this annual renewal is apparent throughout the whole country, Dorset's unique diversity of habitats support a greater range of wildlife than most other English shires.

Between Charmouth and Lyme Regis, the landslip of Black Venn and the Spittles is vulnerable to the constant onslaught of the sea and relentless south-westerly winds. Rocks continuously fall from the cliff and during spells of prolonged wet weather huge mounds of grey, muddy clay spew onto the beach like volcanic larva, leaving behind fissures, which consume shrubs and trees. The very nature of this constantly shifting, hostile landscape makes it truly one of the wildest locations in all of Britain. The dense thickets of scrub on the landslip are teeming with nesting birds. Stonechat, linnet, goldfinch, wren, dunnock and Dartford warbler are all present throughout the year, and will already be incubating their first clutches of eggs.

Motivated by the need to reproduce, and stimulated by lengthening daylight, birds from the south arrive in Dorset to breed. This annual migration has evolved to enable some species to exploit two distinct habitats. In effect, these birds live in perpetual summer, spending winter in warm climates nearer the equator and breeding in the north when daylight hours are extended. The main crop of migrants arrive here on the warm winds of April, when the leaf warblers add their song to the daily clamour of spring. A cascading tumble of minor notes announces the arrival of the willow warbler. Reed beds echo to a melodious concert of reed bunting song, interspersed with loud bursts of anxious chirping from the

PREVIOUS PAGE One of the earliest spring butterflies to be seen this month is the green-veined white.

LEFT Birdsong increases throughout April, reaching a crescendo by the end of the month when the summer migrants arrive. This cock wren is singing to impress his mate with his masculine vocabulary!

RIGHT The hostile landscape of Black Ven; the foreground shows horsetails growing on a mud surge. The cliffs in the background are constantly discharging rocks.

ABOVE Sometimes incorrectly refered to as wild garlic, ramsons thrive in many of Dorset's damp woods and copses, producing a pungent smell similar to garlic during the short flowering period.

LEFT The early purple orchid is the earliest of the common orchids to be seen in the Dorset lanes. Typically it is at its best by the end of April.

Cetti's warbler. In spite of its vociferousness, this small warbler is shy, and rarely breaks cover, delivering its impetuous song while concealed in dense vegetation.

The dawn chorus gathers momentum during April. The transition from night to day affects birdsong as much as the change from winter to summer determines their breeding cycle. More birds sing at dawn in April and May than at any other time. Song continues sporadically throughout the day as individual species spark off spontaneous dialogue with their neighbours. Then there is a final flourish at dusk before Dorset's bird population turns in for the night.

After dark, the sounds of April continue as nocturnal

mammals and birds go about their business. Badger cubs squeak and argue as they timidly explore the world above ground with their parents. They sometimes emerge in daylight, and may be seen near their dens before dusk. Badger cubs are nearly half grown by late April, but stay close to their mother as she teaches them to find food. The badger's preferred diet is earthworms which they feed on for most of the year, but they also have a taste for fruit, and occasionally carrion.

The activities of garden and woodland birds reaches fever pitch as breeding pairs are firmly established and the nesting season gets under way in earnest. Long-tailed tits collect feathers to line their domed lichen nests, while other tits gather moss for their nursery holes. Thrushes often betray the location of their nests by flying in with beaks full of building materials. They are watched keenly by hawk-eyed crows and magpies, who in turn will rob clutches of eggs once they are laid. Nest predation plays a natural and essential role in the intricate balance. Many of the birds which build nests in the shape of cups produce several clutches of eggs throughout the

ABOVE Young badgers start appearing above ground at dusk during April.

BELOW Stonechats occur on the coast, and inland on the Dorset heaths. At this time of year the handsome, black-headed males sing in flight.

ABOVE The main feeding time for the slowworm is after sunset when it hunts seeks slugs and snails especially.

BELOW Although the green-winged orchid is only found at a few sites in Dorset, it can be extremely plentiful, often occurring in great drifts of purple amongst cowslips and dandelions. It can be seen in good numbers at Corfe Mullen and West Bexington

ABOVE The common lizard can be found basking in a sunny spot on April afternoons. As a cold-blooded creature, it needs to regulate its body temperature by moving in and out of the sun.

summer, but only the most carefully concealed nests have a chance of escaping attack. If there were no egg robbers, and the majority of nestlings fledged successfully, there would be insufficient territories or food to sustain such a dramatic population explosion.

The hissing calls of tawny owl fledglings resonate in almost every wood and copse in Dorset as owlets abandon the safety of their nest holes. Young tawny owls leave their nests long before their wing feathers are developed and for several days are flightless. Noisy owlets scattered around in the undergrowth stand a better chance of survival than if they were to remain in the nest together. You occasionally come across them in daylight as scruffy, grey balls of down perched on low branches or even huddled on the ground. This is a natural

stage in their development and they should be given a wide berth, as adult owls will defend their chicks with great determination.

Reptiles also become more active during April as snakes and lizards prepare to breed. As temperatures rise, they move away from their hibernation holes to seek food and potential mates. Snakes prey on other reptiles and small mammals, whereas slowworms and lizards feed principally on insects and spiders. The slowworm is the gardener's ally, for it has particular appetite for the small, white slug *Agriolimax agrestis*, which is a serious pest of tender green vegetables.

Insects are more noticeable in the warm April sunshine as butterflies take to the wing to visit the early flush of spring flowers. The green-veined white butterfly flits along Dorset lanes in its diligent search for food plants on which to lay its

LEFT During the nesting season, the pied wagtail warns off other males by throwing back its head to reveal its black throat-patch and bib.

BELOW Insect-eating birds like the great tit feed on the insects attracted to the April blossom nectar.

eggs. This medium sized, greenish-white butterfly deposits its eggs on garlic mustard and other cruciferous plants.

Pink lady's smock (or milk maids as it is locally known) blooms in old orchards and wet meadows, and attracts spring butterflies. Dog violets flower on roadside banks, their foliage providing food for fritillary butterfly caterpillars. On scrubby banks the early purple orchid pushes up its strong flower spikes, whilst the rare early spider orchid can be seen flowering in the chalky turf along the Purbeck coast. But the plant that makes the most dramatic visual impact on the Dorset countryside is the common dandelion, considered by many an inconvenient weed, but in the wild an important nectar source for hoverflies and honeybees.

If yellow is the predominant colour of verge and meadow, then white is that of the hedgerow. The first trees to blossom are blackthorn and wild cherry, which in turn are followed by hawthorn. Blackthorn can bloom over a long period - from late February to early May in the mildest springs. But when

ABOVE This view of Melplash Court and farmland shows the bright, spring greens of April, back-lit with afternoon sunlight.

cold weather persists, the blossom is retarded, resulting in a sudden explosion of white flowers in April.

The woodland and hedgerow wildflowers of spring have evolved to adapt to conditions dictated by their natural habitat. Dorset, like much of lowland Britain, was once covered in deciduous woodland, so plants like campion, bluebell, stitchwort and bugle developed short, early flowering seasons to coincide with maximum availability of sunlight under trees. As the foliage of deciduous trees opens, and the dark shadow of the canopy smothers the woodland floor, these flowers will have already set seed to complete this stage of their annual cycle. As the leaf buds of beech and oak begin to burst open, the yellow and white gives way to blue as a dense tide of bluebells carpet Dorset's woodlands to herald the arrival of May.

MAY

MAY

O F ALL THE MONTHS, none bursts into life with greater exuberance than May. Nature's seasonal rhythms accelerate as the instinct to reproduce becomes the overriding preoccupation of every plant and animal. Birds sing their intentions from hedge and thicket, while insects flit busily amongst a kaleidoscope of wild flowers.

PREVIOUS PAGE By early May, roe deer have moulted out their mousy, winter fur to don their red summer coats.

BELOW As May progresses, dandelion flowers set seed. This picture was taken in an orchard near Beaminster, just before the winds stripped the dandelion clocks of their parachute seeds.

Dorset is awash with colour as the increase in light and warmth stimulates plants into bloom. Woods are smothered in knee-deep blankets of bluebells. There can be few people who have not stopped to marvel at the spectacle of a wood or copse drenched in a sultry blue haze. Pink drifts of sea thrift adorn the cliffs and coastline, punctuated here and there with a colourful sprinkling of yellow kidney vetch and white sea campion.

In country lanes, the hedge banks are transformed into a rainbow of colour: red campion, ramsons, yellow archangel and the straggly, ground-hugging stems of greater stitchwort. As this annual extravaganza reaches its peak another dramatic performance quickly follows, as Dorset's hedgerows

ABOVE Duncliffe Wood is a Woodland Trust reserve and is particularly spectacular during May, when carpets of bluebells smother the wooded hillside.

are embroidered with creamy white hawthorn blossom.

As dawn breaks, and the drama of spring unfolds, Dorset echoes to a rising tide of birdsong. This is no happy accident of nature, but is the result of millions of years of evolution. Birds have evolved for lightness and flight, with delicate bone structures and fine feathering, and are not suited to physical combat. They therefore generally settle disputes and convey their intentions by displaying and singing.

The songs most synonymous with May are those of the

flying beetles with the sole purpose to mate and lay eggs. Although they actively feed on tree foliage during the day, they only fly at night and are attracted to light – often flying through open windows in a cumbersome but harmless flight.

The main crop of spring butterflies takes to the wing in May, fluttering and gliding amongst the lush vegetation. The holly blue appears like an iridescent, electric-blue flicker as it darts erratically along hedgerows seeking out holly buds on which to lay the first of its two generations of eggs. The

LEFT Red campion is best observed late in the day when low sunshine picks out its hairy stems.

BELOW Also known as cuckoo pint, the arum lily traps insects overnight which unwittingly collect the plant's pollen. The insects are released the following morning and carry the pollen to other plants.

cuckoo and nightingale. The distinctive call of the male cuckoo can be frequently heard throughout the short mating season as he patrols his territory. During the egg laying period he is occasionally answered by the female with an exotic sounding bubbly warble. Female cuckoos lay their eggs in the nests of specific host species and need to locate at least a dozen potential nest sites. In the west of the county they most frequently lay their eggs in dunnock nests, but show a preference for meadow pipits in the east.

A much rarer and more beautiful song is that of the nightingale. Contrary to popular belief, nightingales sing by day as well as at night. The wonderful succession of repeated notes rising to a crescendo - some liquid, some harsh - that characterises their music is best heard in the still of twilight, when males compete for the attentions of females as they arrive from their wintering grounds in Africa. The best places to hear nightingales in Dorset are north of the chalk in the Blackmore Vale; on the Lulworth ranges; and amidst the tangle of hedge, copse and small fields in the Marshwood Vale.

The nightingale's diet includes many of the ground insects that emerge in May to feed on the fresh foliage and pollinate the spring flora. An insect typical of this month is the cockchafer beetle, or maybug. Cockchafers spend their infancy underground as grubs feeding on root crops, often causing significant damage. During May they emerge as large

The first litters of young wild mammals appear above ground to romp or bask peacefully in the warm afternoon sunshine. Fox cubs are frequently seen by day as they play and squabble near their earths, unaware of the hard life of scavenging and hunting that lies ahead. Within the safety of the litter, young cubs learn the art of aggression and defence by play fighting, skills which will prove vital in adulthood. Adult foxes tend to lose condition as the additional pressure of growing cubs forces them to find extra food for their offspring, often at the expense of their own needs.

The Duke of Burgundy fritillary is sadly one of Dorset's declining butterflies. It might still be seen on some of the chalk downs in north-east Dorset.

The orange tip butterfly produces only one generation a year, and is only seen on the wing in adult form during April and May.

orange tip is present for only a few weeks in spring, and throughout May is the most frequently seen butterfly in country lanes, gardens and woodland rides. In flight, the male flashes its bright orange wing tips, but the female lacks the gay patches of orange on the forewing and is not so easy to identify. The orange tip lays its eggs on wayside plants like garlic mustard or lady's smock.

At Powerstock Common the wood white appears as a small, papery butterfly drifting from bloom to bloom. The wood white is typical of coppiced woodland, but is now confined in Dorset to this solitary location, where its numbers continue to hold their own. A succession of other butterflies appear as the month progresses, including both dingy and grizzled skippers, green hairstreak, small copper and speckled wood. Warm southerly winds bring scores of red admirals and painted ladies from the continent. These two flamboyantly coloured species rely upon migration to breed here, as they are unable to survive the winter in Dorset.

The Duke of Burgundy fritillary also hatches towards the end of the month. Once a fairly common species in Dorset, occurring in light woodland and on scrubby slopes with lush ground cover, it has sadly declined to a point where it is now absent from many of its former haunts. It may still be seen on Fontmell Down, where a dwindling population maintains a tenuous toehold. The females lay their eggs on the cowslips that carpet the slopes of the down.

Blue tits feed their nestlings on the caterpillars of the winter moth.

The majority of our summer birds have well-established breeding territories by early May. The county's reed beds come alive with a melodious concert of incessant, frantic songs, revealing the presence of sedge and reed warblers. Both these tiny birds will have made the treacherous migration flight from Africa in order to nest and rear their young. Elsewhere along the coast the distinct chattering of terns adds to the summery atmosphere. These birds, often called sea swallows, live on a diet of small fish, diving headlong into the water to catch them. Sandwich and common terns are first seen in the Fleet lagoon, later dispersing to their breeding grounds at Lodmoor and Brownsea Island.

By the end of May, the last of the migrants will have arrived. The spotted flycatcher is a creature of habit, often returning to the same nesting site in creepers on a wall or tree and discreetly taking up residence as if it had never been

ABOVE Green woodpeckers feed their nestlings exclusively on ant eggs, which they regurgitate at the nest.

OPPOSITE PAGE Owls are early nesters and this little owl, photographed near Mangerton was bringing in earthworms and moths at twilight to feed its hungry owlets.

ABOVE Common terns have established their nest sites at Lodmoor and Brownsea by early May.

BELOW Adult foxes are frequently seen out hunting in daylight in May because they have additional mouths to feed.

ABOVE The area round Knowlton Church is rich in unusual wild flowers, including knapweed broomrape and fragrant orchids.

BELOW In early May, the viridescent green hue of new beech leaves makes its annual debut along the avenue near Badbury Rings.

LEFT Young stoats run with their mothers for a few days and may be seen romping and fighting. Stoats are likely to be present wherever extensive rabbit colonies occur in open countryside.

away. Another bird to annually make the three thousand mile journey from Africa is the swift. Swifts only land when they nest; the rest of their lives are spent entirely on the wing. Swifts take two years to become sexually mature, so a first time breeding bird will have flown non-stop for two years!

By the end of the month the bluebell flowers have faded into swollen seedpods, leaving other wild plants to take centre stage. Buttercups, foxgloves and a procession of orchids appear to mark the final transition from spring to summer.

JUNE

JUNE

The advent of summer is epitomised by village fêtes and droning lawnmowers, by growth and abundance and sweet-smelling perfumes. The sky barely darkens at night and dawn comes early, the warm sun sailing high long before many of us of stir. In Dorset's copses and spinneys, woodland birds continue to hatch second and even third broods. Wrens blurt out their noisy chorus and the quick, hurried jingle of the blackcap echoes enigmatically amongst brambles and rose briers. On downland in the heart of the county, a curious rattle of tinkling notes is recited by the corn bunting, and from gorse and hedgetop the cock yellow-hammer pours out his repetitive lilt.

Along the coast, the strident cries of young gulls, fulmars and other seabirds are heard above the rumbling waves. Peregrines fledge from their eyries on Purbeck, Portland and the higher sea cliffs of the west. These immature falcons are frequently taken on training flights with their parents. The keen-eyed peregrine lives on a diet of pigeons and doves, and in a dive can reach speeds of up to 180mph. Surprisingly, the peregrine's only enemy is the fulmar, whose defence technique is to spit at potential enemies. A peregrine, perching near a nesting fulmar, risks being splattered by glutinous vomit, which can congeal on the plumage and prevent the falcon from flying.

A cacophony of calls and alarm notes emit from the tern colonies of Weymouth and Brownsea as adults fly in with fish. The rarest of the tern family in Dorset is the little tern, which breeds annually at the Ferrybridge end of Chesil Beach. The numbers of this blackbird-sized tern have been declining for

PREVIOUS PAGE Early June in the Marshwood Vale, where every hedge and tree is now in full leaf.

RIGHT Young peregrines leave their nests in June, when they may be seen sitting on rock outcrops at West Bay or Portland. They are frequently taken on training flights and taught to hunt by their parents.

ABOVE The little tern (about the size of a blackbird) nests in a colony on the Chesil Beach at Ferrybridge each year.

RIGHT The broad-bodied chaser is the earliest of the common dragonflies to appear. The females hatch from the aquatic nymph stage several days before the males, thus allowing them to dry their wings and become airborne before amorous males are present.

years. They nest on exposed sites on the shingle, and are at risk from sudden freak storms and predators such as gulls and foxes. Even hedgehogs have been known to make the perilous journey out over the shingle to take their eggs and dependent young.

On inland waters, the first of the dragonflies hatch and take to the air to feed on airborne insects. Male broad-bodied and four-spotted chasers wait like sentries on favoured perches to dart out at intruders. The emperor, Europe's largest dragonfly, tirelessly patrols his breeding domain, and on

quick-flowing streams the beautiful demoiselle dances over the water.

Young mink venture along the rivers, robbing vulnerable ducklings and other riverbank creatures of their lives. Mink are not native to Britain but became established after escaping from mink farms during the last century. These indiscriminate, vicious hunters were once a scourge, decimating populations of watervoles, birds and fish. The successful return of the otter to Dorset will hopefully bring about a welcome decline in the mink population, as the larger otter will not put up with mink within its territory.

Another resident of Dorset's rivers is the kingfisher. The young leave their nests in June, and the patient spectator might be rewarded by the wonderful aquamarine flash of a kingfisher in flight. The juveniles are tolerated for only a few days before they are abandoned and evicted from the breeding territory. This is a crucial time: the angle and judgement of a dive is critical, and a high percentage of immature birds drown in their first attempts to catch fish.

At about this time, the first fledgling swallows also make

ABOVE After a long absence, the otter has returned to Dorset, but it is seldom seen as it is mainly nocturnal and very secretive.

their maiden flights, and for a few days are vulnerable to attacks by predators. They are easy prey for the sparrowhawk and hobby and are supervised closely by their anxious parents. They are fed as they wait patiently, clinging to wires, and for several days return at dusk to roost in the old nest.

On south-facing hillsides where generations of ants have constructed large fortresses, jays stir up the nests and crouch with wings spread to encourage the insects to crawl into their plumage. Ants exude toxins like formic acid in defence of their nests, and such poisons are very effective against other insects, thus helping to reduce parasites living within the jay's own plumage - a kind of insecticidal shampoo!

Many insects hatch or emerge in the increasing warmth, including grasshoppers and crickets resembling miniature versions of their parents. The pupal stage, typical of insect metamorphosis, is missing in both families. They develop through a series of stages before reaching sexual maturity.

ABOVE A young swallow calls to its parents for food.

RIGHT The lesser spotted is the smallest and least common of Dorset's woodpeckers. This male was returning to its nest in an apple tree near Brackets Coppice Nature Reserve, Halstock.

Ringlet and large skipper butterflies appear in the hedgerows, and on the downs the Adonis blue lays its eggs on horse-shoe vetch. The small pearl-bordered fritillary flies along woodland glades and across rough pasture, settling in the warmth of the sun to display its exquisite wing markings. The richly coloured marsh fritillary lays its eggs on Devil's bit scabious and is now confined to only a couple of sites in Dorset.

On the heaths, the wealth of insects provide rich pickings for meadow pipits and Dartford warblers, both with hungry young to feed. Meadow pipits erupt from the heather in spectacular song flights, culminating in impressive parachute displays as they float back down to the ground on quivering wings. Male cuckoos continue to call on the heaths until late in the month. Once egg production is complete, they feed

voraciously in preparation for their long return migration flight.

At dusk, as other birds fall silent, the nightjar sings from a favourite perch. At first a soft, droning purr rises to a mechanical chirring, similar to the sound of a sewing machine. The song is interrupted with abrupt cracks of wing clapping as the males take flight. These extraordinary birds are active after sunset, swooping over the heather in the dim twilight to catch moths.

Dorset is one of the few counties in Britain which supports healthy populations of all six native reptiles. In June these

cold-blooded creatures are active during the day. Overnight their blood temperatures cool and they need to heat up again after dawn by lying in the open to absorb warmth from the sun. Typically, reptiles bask at both ends of the day to regulate their body temperatures. The smooth snake exists on a diet of lizards and other small reptiles and basks on sandy heath banks. It is Britain's rarest native reptile, and maintains a national stronghold on the heaths of Dorset and Hampshire.

Dorset's most unusual reptile occurs in old quarry workings on the Isle of Portland. The Iberian wall lizard is thought to have arrived on Portland via boats collecting stone. It has bred on the island for at least 30 years and has colonies in both Tout and Cheyne Weares quarries.

ABOVE The smooth snake owes its name to its scales, which unlike other reptiles are smooth with no keel or ridge.

BELOW The fresh green shoots of maize emerge in meandering lines across a field near Hardy's Monument in early June.

OPPOSITE PAGE TOP The small pearl-borderd fritillary may still be seen on Powerstock Common throughout June.

OPPOSITE PAGE BELOW Birdsong continues throughout June as species like the blackcap rear second or even third broods of young.

ABOVE The flowers of the bee orchid mimick the bodies of bees in order to attract the insects for pollination.

LEFT Water crowfoot floats in the shallows of the River Frome, near Dorchester.

Away from the windswept heights of Portland, with its thin limestone soil, Dorset's fields and haymeadows are carpeted with buttercups. Tiers of elder blossom cascade from the hedgerows. Ragged robin and flag iris bloom in the watermeadows and oxeye daisies flower along roadside banks. Frothy sprays of delicate cow parsley grace country lanes; its billowing blooms affectionately known as 'Queen Anne's lace'.

June is the best month for orchids, a bewitching group of wild flowers. The common spotted orchid is the most

plentiful, particularly on undisturbed roadside verges. Heath spotted orchids poke through the budding heather, and the showy, southern marsh orchid proudly blooms in damp pasture. Rarities of this family include the lizard orchid, which occurs on the roadside verge at Slepe and is at its prime in June. Bee and butterfly orchids are found throughout the county, and are most abundant on chalk downland. In mature oak woodlands the curious birds nest orchid rises from the leaf litter, usually where few other plants can tolerate the deep shade.

ABOVE Honeybees typically swarm in June, as the old queen leaves the nest with thousands of workers to start a new colony.

JULY

JULY

On warm evenings, shoals of midges drift and linger in the air, and the humming of bumblebees continues past sunset. The effects of change are most significant in the sounds of this gentlest of months. Voices and laughter carry across the countryside until well after dark, and birdsong gives way to a continuous drone of insects

With the nesting season almost over, many birds gradually fall silent. In the evenings yellowhammer and whitethroat occasionally twitter quietly in the lanes, and robins argue over their new, solitary territories, singing quietly at each other.

On farmland throughout the county, young buzzards incessantly call, demanding food. Adult buzzards provide their fledglings with a regular supply of small rodents and it is not unusual to observe the tumbling flight of two juveniles locked together, grappling over some tasty morsel.

July marks the beginning of a new phase in the annual cycle of birds, as the summer moult replaces tired plumage, tattered and worn by the ravages of rearing young. Most birds simultaneously moult two feathers from each wing, impairing

their flying, so they tend to hide during this process. At a time of year when there are more birds in Dorset than any other, we actually see little evidence of them. The annual summer moult continues through to early September, neatly coinciding with an abundance of food. Large birds like geese and swans are flightless during the moult, and for safety remain close to water where they can seek refuge from a prowling fox. At Abbotsbury Swannery, this period is used for the biennial round up of the swans. At first light, hundreds of volunteers quietly wade into the water to surround the birds and gently

PREVIOUS PAGE The whitethroat is one of the last birds to sing in the Dorset lanes. Typically, the song of this summer warbler is scratchy and erratic.

BELOW LEFT A buzzard with its prey. The adults are kept busy throughout July providing their young with food.

BELOW The marbled white is one of the most prolific butterflies to be seen this month. Often building up huge colonies even when confined to a roadside verge.

ABOVE During the peak of the moulting season, swans (like geese) become flightless. At Abbotsbury, this is the time for the biennial swan round up when all the swans are weighed and their health is checked.

herd them towards a catchment pen. Here each swan is weighed and given a thorough health check before being released back onto the Fleet.

July is the most active month for insects. Dorset is renowned for its diverse range of butterflies and dragonflies. On chalk downland, common blue butterflies flit between the knapweeds, sipping nectar for energy, while on the heaths the silver studded blue comes on the wing. The slow flying marbled white is a distinctive butterfly with a chequered appearance, frequently visiting thistle and scabious flowers throughout July. Large colonies are typically found on unimproved grassland on well-drained chalk or limestone soils. Their sedentary nature also allows them to thrive in quite small colonies on roadside banks and central reservations.

In the oakwoods of Dorset, silver washed fritillaries feed on bramble flowers from around the third week of the month, and large clusters of peacock caterpillars strip nettles of their leaves before pupating. Dorset has its own butterfly species, the Lulworth skipper, which occurs along the coast between Weymouth and Swanage in remarkably large colonies. It was first recorded at Durdle Door in 1832, and is thought to be one of the few species of butterfly currently on the increase.

ABOVE The silver-studded blue is abundant on the Dorset heaths in early July where it lays its eggs on gorse and broom.

ABOVE Horses and cattle graze the lush grasses of Stanpit Marsh, Christchurch.

Many of the mid-summer dragonflies hatch in July, including ruddy and black darters, which both prefer the acidic ponds and bogs of the heath. In the evenings, predatory hawker dragonflies feast upon rising swarms of gnats and midges. Dragonfly legs are lined with stiff bristles to aid the catching of food in flight. Their three pairs of legs are held in front to form a basket in which the prey is caught. Most small flies are consumed on the wing, but larger insects are taken to a perch to be dismembered and eaten.

The bee-killer, or bee-wolf as it is popularly known, is a digger wasp and a relatively newcomer to Dorset. Previously recorded as an occasional migrant from Europe, it now breeds at Winfrith and Stoborough heaths as well as at a number of other sites. The adult wasp excavates a system of tunnels in sandy banks and lays its eggs in nursery chambers. It preys upon honeybees, which are carried in flight, slung upside-down under the wasp's body. The dead bees are pushed into the tunnels for the wasp grubs to feed on when they hatch.

On Dorset's heaths, the first of a succession of heathers bring colour to the drab moorlands. Reddish-purple blooms

RIGHT The male banded demoiselle displays distinctive wing patches of deep purple.

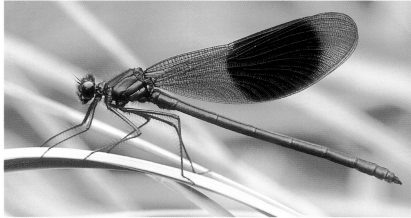

of bell heather mingle with the rose pink of cross- leaved heath, giving off an intoxicating scent to attract bumblebees and hoverflies. Elsewhere, the flowering of Dorset continues with lavish displays of sow-thistle, knapweed, great willowherb and tangled, unkempt knots of tufted vetch and yellow mellilot. Blood-red poppies magically appear on roadside verges where they have never previously flowered. The gypsy lifestyle of the field poppy is linked to its main habitat requirement - disturbed ground, where the earth has been completely turned over.

OPPOSITE PAGE TOP The old quarry workings at Tout Quarry on Portland are home to a wide range of lime-loving wild flowers.

OPPOSITE PAGE BOTTOM Looking towards Compton Vallence. The summer harvest dramatically changes the look of the countryside, as wheat and barley are cut and baled straw left to dry.

ABOVE Sundews grow in the acid bogs of heathland. They are insectivorous plants and gain nutrients from insects, which become trapped on their sticky leaves.

RIGHT Weld and viper's buglos, both of which can be seen along the Purbeck coast, and are particularly abundant on the Island of Portland.

The chalk escarpment, which stretches diagonally from the north-east to the southwest, supports prolific colonies of wild flowers, particularly where steep hillsides have made ploughing impossible. These herb rich slopes are at their best in July, with locally abundant species such as kidney vetch, salad burnet, hoary plantain, wild thyme and common rockrose. The delicate blooms of the carline thistle resemble little more than dry seedheads at first glance. Clustered bellflower, autumn gentian and sawort are all species seldom seen far from the chalk hills, as are the purple and yellow flowers of ploughman's spikenard. This soft biennial derives its name from its fragrant roots, which are only savoured when the plant is disturbed – as by ploughing.

As hay meadow wild flowers fade and set seed, country lanes across Dorset are busy with the hectic toing and froing of combine harvesters and tractors hauling trailers laden with grain. Formations of round bales, scattered like giant draught pieces, appear where only a few days earlier fields of wheat and barley had been ripening. In the fields around Chideock and North Poorton, long straw wheat is cut with antiquated binder machines for the local thatching trade. The traditional wheatsheaf stooks, relics of a bygone age, are left to dry in the fields, and are later thrashed to separate the wheat from the chaff.

ABOVE The sand lizard is arguably Dorset's most beautiful reptile. This female was found basking on a sandy bank at Higher Hyde Heath.

LEFT Unlike other reptiles the grass snake does not give birth to live young, but lays eggs in decaying organic matter, which generates warmth for incubation. As a result, grass snakes are often encountered on or near compost heaps during July.

In the warmth of high summer, reptiles give birth to live young. Only grass snakes lay eggs, which are deposited in decaying organic matter, because as cold-blooded creatures they are unable to continue incubation when their bodies cool down at night. Typically, eggs are laid in compost heaps where they are incubated by the warmth generated by decomposition.

Dorset's mammals add ripening nuts and fruits to their diet. In broad-leaved woodland, squirrels strip bark from field maple, oak, beech and sycamore. This destructive behaviour is common when squirrel population densities are at their highest. It is thought the squirrel is seeking the nutrient rich vascular tissue, which lies beneath the bark.

In secluded meadows, roe deer bring their fawns out in the open to graze in the evening sunshine. While the doe keeps a watchful eye on her young, the buck becomes bold and frisky, as the rutting season is imminent. In dry weather, badgers, unable to dig for earthworms, turn their attention to soft fruit in gardens, even upending dustbins in their desperate search for food.

By the end of the month, although the shortening evenings are hardly yet noticeable, hills like the Purbecks and the rolling heights of Cranborne Chase shimmer in the heat haze. On humid nights, bats fly with rapid wingbeats to feed on a nocturnal horde of moths and other insects. Prolonged warm conditions bring an increasing threat of thunder, that untamed peculiarity of high summer.

ABOVE A great spotted woodpecker feeding a fledgeling. The young woodpecker will lose its crimson cap after the summer moult.

BELOW This handsome lichen (*Cladonia Apothecia*) displays clusters of bright red spore-producing caps and can be found on dry heathland in summer.

Roe deer fawns are usually born in June, but by July they are
becoming more independent, as the adults grow restless at the
onset of the rut.

AUGUST

AUGUST

There is a sense of weariness in the browning Dorset countryside as the lushness of summer begins to fade. It is August, the quiet interlude between the seasons of renewal and those of decline. The air can be oppressive and sultry; a constant murmur of buzzing insects the only evidence of animated life. In the stillness, butterflies float on tissue paper wings and hawker dragonflies hover and glide along country lanes like miniature helicopters.

The rich variety of dragonfly species in Dorset is due to the county's wonderful range of habitats. Some of these predatory insects prefer fast-flowing streams; some seek out ponds and lakes; whilst others thrive in the acidic bogs of the lowland heaths in the south-east. Dragonflies are primitive insects, which were fully evolved around the time of the dinosaurs. Some of the large, impressive hawker dragonflies typical of August include the golden ringed, migrant and southern hawkers.

On the open moors of Hartland, Studland and Godlingston heaths common hawkers persistently patrol the bogs and ponds. The dragonflies of the heaths are the most numerous, and in turn they attract the attention of the hobby. This small falcon snatches dragonflies with alacrity, deftly picking off the wings and eating their bodies in flight. There can be few more exhilarating sights than watching a hobby catching dragonflies over a heathland bog, as it swoops and dives with deadly accuracy in pursuit of a quarry that is itself both fast and erratic.

The proliferation of high summer butterflies peaks in August with the emergence of several notably abundant species. The meadow brown, Britain's commonest butterfly, occurs in hedgerows and fields, feeding on thistles and scabious along with the smaller but also common gatekeeper. Red admiral, painted lady, peacock and small tortoiseshell butterflies visit gardens to sip the nectar of buddleia, sedum and catmint flowers.

PREVIOUS PAGE Crickets lack the pupal stage, common in most insects. Instead, they develop through a series of nymphal stages. Here a cricket is shown wriggling from its outer skin as it passes between stages.

ABOVE Dorset has long been a stronghold for the hobby. In August it begins to feed on dragonflies and other large insects, which it takes on the wing.

ABOVE The heathers bring colour to Godlingston Heath in late summer.

RIGHT The bell heather is one of the commonest of the Dorset heathers. At the beginning of August it will be at its best as it smothers the county's heathlands.

On the north Dorset hills, silver spotted skipper, brown argus and common blue busily feed on the chalk downland flowers like dwarf thistle and vetches. Occasionally, meeting one of their own kind, they dizzily waltz around each other in a brief courtship dance, until the female lands to suggestively raise her abdomen.

Chalkhill blues flutter amongst the vetches on sunny afternoons and clouded yellows dart across the downs in a brisk meandering flight. The clouded yellow is the nomad of Dorset's butterflies, hardly noticed for years until a sudden increase in numbers migrating from the continent make it one

of the most striking insects to be seen on the downs.

The elusive, fast flying grayling is specific to heathland, appearing as a large, colourful butterfly in flight, but when at rest it is the master of disguise. The grayling closes its wings to conceal the conspicuous eyespots, revealing a motley, camouflaged pattern of grey, brown, black and white to the undersides. When sunning itself on the ground, it tilts its closed wings away from the sun, thus reducing tell-tale shadows and making it remarkably difficult to locate.

A butterfly more usually associated with early spring than high summer is the brimstone, which seldom opens its wings when at rest. The brimstones seen in the Dorset lanes next March and April hatch as adult butterflies in August, feeding on thistle flowers in late summer. The unusual shape of its wings enables it to hibernate in evergreen foliage during the winter.

An eye-catching insect, which has become increasingly common in recent years, is the hummingbird hawkmoth. It flies by day, hovering to dip its long proboscis deep into buddliea, verbena or valerian flowers. It arrives here in spring from southern Europe, and although it breeds in Dorset is unable to survive our winters.

The wild flower season reaches its spectacular finale in August as more heathers come into bloom on the heathlands of east Dorset. Ling, the commonest member of the heather family, now joins cross-leaved heath and bell heather. But the county has its very own heather species, the Dorset heath, which is particularly abundant on Hartland Moor. First impressions are of a deep pink bell heather, but its structure is different and the flowers are borne on tall spikes. Elsewhere the final explosion of colour is delivered by rosebay willowherb, whose lofty, pink spires line roadside banks.

TOP Brimstone butterflies simply cannot resist the nectar of spear thistle flowers. This is a newly hatched insect in early August, and is one of a few butterflies which exist in adult form for almost a whole year.

CENTRE The mottled markings of the grayling enable the insect to practically vanish as it comes to rest on the sand. Here a pair are shown mating in the heather.

BOTTOM Second generation painted lady butterflies emerge in August. This is a common butterfly in gardens where it visits catmint, sedum and verbena flowers.

conducted around a tree or bush. The buck chases the doe around this central point, their hooves wearing a distinct ring in the ground. Mating and fertilization take place inside the ring, but implantation of the embryo is delayed until December, and the young, generally twins, are born the following May or June.

Birds continue to remain silent throughout the month while they complete the moulting process. The curiously marked birds that appear in gardens are the current year's crop of fledgelings, which have not yet matured into full adult plumage. Tinkling charms of juvenile goldfinches, devoid of red balaclavas, feed on thistle down and dandelion seeds; and drab, colourless bullfinches seek the seed of docks and nettles.

LEFT The pink spires of rosebay willowherb occur in dense troops on roadside verges.

BELOW The tiny autumn gentian can be seen on chalk downland throughout the north of the county in August.

By now, young mammals are dispersing; leaving the familiar landscape where they were born to make their own way in the world. Badger cubs adopt a noticeably more serious attitude and young foxes lope around the meadows and hedgerows like gangling teenagers. Foxes have a high mortality rate and few of this season's young will survive beyond their first year.

High summer is the mating season for some mammals, and the annual rut of the county's roe deer takes place in August. Numbers of all species of deer in Dorset are on the increase, and what was once a rare sight is now increasingly common. The rut usually takes place in woodland, where courtship is

OPPOSITE PAGE An old fashioned strain of wheat is grown for its long straw, which is harvested for the thatching trade. Here, the sheafs are left in the fields to dry, and decorate the landscape at Chideock.

ABOVE The splendid hummingbird hawkmoth arrives here from southern Europe in spring. By August, its numbers usually have increased and it can be quite common in gardens.

Fledgeling kingfishers, with short beaks and dull plumage, can be seen near garden ponds. This behaviour is due to a population increase caused by an overflow of youngsters, who have been driven from their parents' territories.

Swallows and martins congregate in the villages to moult their feathers in readiness for the hazardous journey south. They sit preening on wires, twittering incessantly and frequently erupting in sudden explosive flights. Eventually, these dummy runs come to an end, the wires are suddenly empty, and they will not be seen again until the following spring. An unwelcome companion is the hobby, having given

BELOW The approach road to the village of Moor Crichel near Witchampton is lined with young beech trees. The lower branches have been 'brashed', giving the impression of a row of lollipops!

OPPOSITE PAGE TOP The young little grebe adopts a submissive attitude as its parent approaches with a fish.

OPPOSITE PAGE BOTTOM Throughout the moult, birds spend much time preening and bathing. Here, an adult songthrush bathes enthusiastically in a garden pond.

RIGHT An adult female kingfisher, droops her wings and sways from side to side in an aggressive manner to drive off one of her own youngsters.

up chasing dragonflies in favour of swallows and martins. The hobby is a summer visitor and also flies south for the winter, feeding on immature swallows and martins during the journey.

As the succession of wild flowers go to seed, so the summer fruits ripen to provide an important supply of food for many wild creatures. Blackberries offer nourishment to a wide range of insects, mammals and birds. Comma and red admiral butterflies sip the juices from the ripening fruits, which are popular with blackbirds and woodmice; whilst blackcaps and thrushes feed on the oval berries of woody nightshade and the red honeysuckle fruits.

By the end of the month, flurries of delicate thistledown seeds glide and linger in the faintest breeze. Bracken fronds begin to turn yellow; a clear reminder that August is the last, full month of summer.

The lost valley of Tyneham has been devoid of human inhabitants since the Second World War, when the army evicted the population to use the area for training. The valley has remained under military control ever since, and as a result is a haven for wildlife.

SEPTEMBER

SEPTEMBER

Shades of autumn creep in around the edges as September begins. Change is in the air. The days may be warm, but evening temperatures progressively drop lower. In the cool mornings, thin layers of mist drift wispily over the stubble fields, and the first traces of fog are draped across rivers and ponds. Willowherb seeds stand erect and swollen, and Indian balsam flowers hang still as silent bells, their seedpods laden with moisture.

On heaths and commons, every bush, shrub and briar is clothed in a tapestry of dangling spider webs. Each individual net of gossamer is a unique feat of engineering and one of nature's most remarkable achievements. Many spiders have evolved their adult stage to coincide with autumn, when there is a wealth of potential food. The web-making spiders are amongst only a handful of animals in the world which build traps to catch their prey. Cobwebs are constructed late in the

PREVIOUS PAGE Small mammals collect food for winter storage. The woodmouse is a skilful climber, and will carry nuts and berries back to its food store.

BELOW Lit up by early morning sunlight, a spider stands at the centre of its web.

September is the most typical month for the wryneck to turn up in Dorset. These strange little birds feed on ants and their grubs which they search for in short turf.

Small waders like the common sandpiper turn up at inland lakes and ponds in September as they move through Dorset at the start of the autumn migration.

day, ready for operation the following morning, when lethargic, airborne insects are more likely to blunder into them.

There is renewed activity amongst birds. The summer moult complete, they become more conspicuous as they feed on the harvest of nuts, seeds and fruit. Restless migrants begin to gravitate towards Portland. The southernmost tip of the island protrudes eight miles into the English Channel, making it one of the most important bird migration highways in Britain. The summer visitors depart in droves, including the martins and swallows, most of the warblers, the terns and some of the specialist heathland species like nightjar and hobby.

Other migrants passing through Dorset include common sandpiper and wryneck. The sandpiper is a small wader, which frequents inland lakes and rocky streams, where it feeds on invertebrates. In most years the wryneck turns up sporadically in the south of the county to feed on garden lawns. This curious little bird is classified as a member of the

woodpecker family, and feeds mainly on ants and their grubs. It owes its name to the extraordinary twisting postures it adopts during courtship and threat display. On undisturbed lawns where ants are abundant, it may remain feeding for several days before resuming its journey to north-west Africa.

Happily, bird migration works in both directions. As the summer visitors leave, so the winter waders start to arrive. Black tailed godwits fly in from eastern Europe and Iceland to gather at Lodmoor and Ferrybridge, and avocets begin to appear in the Brownsea lagoon. At the same time, purple sandpipers arrive on the coast from their Arctic breeding quarters to spend winter on the rocks of Portland and the Cobb at Lyme Regis.

Inland, on hedge and thicket, there is a ripening harvest of nuts and berries. In the warmth of late summer, this is nature's final offering before autumn sets in. There is a rustling in the coppices as grey squirrels clamber amongst the branches to pluck ripening hazelnuts from their ragged cups. Hazelnuts are also eaten by dormice, woodmice and that specialist

ABOVE Grey squirrels and pheasants eat horse chestnuts, but those which are overlooked remain buried in the leaf litter to germinate the following spring.

LEFT The fluffy seed heads of traveller's joy, or old man's beard make an impressive display at the end of summer.

ABOVE On Brownsea Island the delightful red squirrel can be seen busily collecting nuts for winter storage this month.

nutcracker - the nuthatch. This smart woodland bird, distinguished by its black eye stripe and white throat, wedges hazelnuts into crevices, then cracks the casing with its sharply pointed 'hatchet' beak. The dormouse is more fastidious, cutting a neat, spherical hole to get at the kernel; woodmice make irregular, untidy incisions; whilst grey squirrels tend to split the nuts directly in half. The red squirrels of Brownsea Island busily gather sweet chestnuts and pine cones, which they carry off to hide in their secret winter larders.

Along the hedgerows, hips of wild roses start to redden, and shiny black elderberries hang in dense clusters. Elderberries are consumed with enthusiasm by a wide variety of birds, including blackcap, robin, blackbird and woodpigeon. Once the red rowan berries ripen they are quickly taken by bullfinches and thrushes. The tortuous sprawling route taken by bryony as it grew is now finally revealed by its bloated fruits. Poisonous to humans, the berries display attractive colours, ranging from greens and yellows to rich crimson. Old man's beard or travellers joy scrambles over shrubs and hedges to unfurl its fluffy seed heads in a final, spectacular flourish.

A liberal dosing of September rain, coupled with the seasonal warmth, can produce ideal humid conditions for the first toadstools. On pasture land the white button caps of field mushrooms appear overnight in fairy rings, and the large, elegant parasol toadstool, decorated with shaggy scales, emerges to release its spores.

PREVIOUS PAGES As the sun rises over Buckland Newton, for a brief moment the landscape is tinted with shades of orange.

ABOVE The beach huts lining Christchurch Harbour form a colourful backdrop for the large numbers of wading birds which arrive in September to spend winter in the Harbour, a mecca for bird lovers in the far east of the county.

OPPOSITE PAGE TOP The venerable oaks of Powerstock Common exhibit hoary, grizzled knuckles and twisted branches.

OPPOSITE PAGE BOTTOM Hundreds of gulls and other water birds gather within the safety of the RSPB reserve at Radipole Lake.

On Lewesdon Hill, the beechwood is sombre under the heavy canopy. Leaves hang in drab shades of green and the vegetation on the ground seems shabby and abandoned. Occasional squeaks betray the presence of parties of tits feeding in the canopy. The pathetic, mewing cries of fledgeling buzzards echoes through the wood as they sail the skies with their parents. Buzzards, like crows and black-headed gulls, have learned to exploit the plough. As the stubble fields are ploughed and drilled with winter wheat, they follow the tractor in search of churned up insects and molluscs.

On the coast, clumps of eyebright persist with their tiny cheerful flowers, and the yellow blooms of horn poppy fade into long seedpods. Sea holly shows off the last of its powdery blue flowers, which are protected by vicious spiky leaves. In the muddy, salt marshes of Poole and Christchurch harbours, sea lavender continues to flower in thick swathes of pink blooms.

Through woods and fields, seeds of the next generation of plants float by on feathery parachutes, drifting and falling, the offspring of their decaying parents. The blue of devil's bit scabious contrasts with the vibrant yellows of fleabane and marsh ragwort. On verges and waste ground, the evening primrose daily produces new fresh flowers.

The last few hardy swallows swoop low over meadows and ponds to prey upon troops of mosquitoes. Their offspring already departed, these adult birds will remain until the first frosts decimate the insect population.

The grey heron, patient killer of the marshes, stands motionless in knee-deep water, occasionally swivelling its pickaxe bill. It stares straight down at the water with its yellow eyee, searching for the tiniest ripple likely to reveal the movement of potential food. Finally, it slowly bends forward, its long neck doubles like a spring, and then it strikes, its beak stabbing with lightning speed to seize a hapless stickleback.

ABOVE The comma (so named because of a white comma shape on the underside of the wing) is especially fond of the juice of ripening blackberries.

LEFT This elderly example of a common darter dragonfly has completely lost its breeding colours.

One insect that might distract even the most patient heron is the empid fly, which in late summer performs an aerial courtship display over Dorset's rivers. Tens of thousands of males form a drifting cloud, which floats above the water to attract females. The male then lures the female with a gift of a silk-wrapped parcel of prey, from which she sucks the juices as the male mates with her.

Autumn is on its way, the season of decline and decay. The first acorns start to drop and silver birch leaves turn brown and yellow. The final transition from abundance to depletion is about to begin.

OCTOBER

OCTOBER

October drifts in on a thickening mist, which curls through the woods and hollows, and hangs suspended above low lying fields. Silhouettes are softened and beads of silvery moisture sparkle in the thistledown and decorate spiders' webs like strings of pearls. In the woods, the early sun glances through the fading canopy. The late summer silence is interrupted by the contact calls of tits and finches and the frantic scurrying of creatures in the undergrowth as wildlife prepares for winter.

Of all the Dorset seasons, autumn is the shortest. But it is nonetheless spectacular, as deciduous trees turn from green to gold, ushering in the most sudden transformation of the year. The broad-leaved woods begin the month in the sombre, dark greens of late summer, and end it in a final flourish of resplendent autumn colour. First to change are the birches, followed by horse chestnut and field maple. Later, ash and beech turn brown and yellow; only the stubborn oak retaining its greenery until well into November. These fiery autumn colours are no happy accident of nature. Deciduous trees spend the summer building up tissues for new cell growth through the process of photosynthesis. As trees enter the dormant season, pigments are broken down and soluble products are transported back into the branches for winter storage. The remaining degraded pigments of redundant leaves produce the glorious hues of autumn.

PREVIOUS PAGE In the east of the county, the fly agaric toadstool occurs along rides and in woods during October. The white spots on the crimson cap are the shrivelled remains of a veil, which protected the fruiting body as it pushed its way up through the earth.

RIGHT Some species of fungi like the sulphur tuft, can produce troops of hundreds of toadstools on a single tree trunk. This fungus is very common, occurring in woods and copses throughout Dorset at this time of year.

ABOVE   Trooping crumple cap is a common fungus, often producing dense troops of delicate toadstools.

In the moisture-laden air, an army of toadstools appear as delicate pedestals rising from the leaf litter, or festooned on both dead and living wood. Fungus, like moss, appears without warning in all its glory, at a time when everything else is dying back. In a wet, humid October, a huge variety can emerge literally overnight, many assuming extraordinary shapes. Some are colourful and attractive, others are culinary delights, and a few are deadly poisonous. The most familiar group are the toadstools, releasing their life-giving spores from slits or gills beneath protective umbrella caps. The most poisonous, the aptly named death cap, grows near old oak trees on Powerstock Common, and in Duncliffe Wood and Brackets Coppice.

As October progresses, late afternoon sunlight picks out tumbledown bracken fronds amongst the dark pines of Wareham Forest. Columns of gnats dangle in the shafting sunbeams. Late insects dart in and out of the lengthening shadows. Many continue to fly until their activities are curtailed by the first frosts. Bumblebees and hover flies enjoy the late summer flowers, a final indulgence of nectar before winter sets in. Wasps and honeybees continue their work,

ABOVE LEFT Southern hawker dragonflies patrol country lanes on warm October days.

ABOVE Red admirals feed on the juices of over-ripe fruit in autumn. Most of these colourful butterflies die off during winter though, and are replenished by migrants arriving here from southern Europe in spring.

LEFT Goldfinches feed on the ripening seeds of teasel, combing the seedheads with the sides of their beaks to loosen the seeds.

seemingly oblivious to the gathering mood of change. Southern hawker dragonflies patrol woodland rides and ponds. This is the last of the large hawker dragonflies of the year, and may well be flying as late as mid-November. The success of the southern hawker is due to its willingness to share the breeding habitat. A male will guard a breeding pond until challenged by another male, which it then leaves to the newcomer, thus operating a kind of time-share scheme.

All around the county, wildlife continues to reap the autumn harvest. Squirrels and jays collect nuts for winter storage and red admiral butterflies and other late insects sip the juices of over-ripe fruit. Along the hedgerows handsome goldfinches harvest seed from thickets of teasels or sway on downy thistles. In the woods, acorns rain down, to be swallowed whole by pheasants or eaten by deer browsing the understorey vegetation. Squirrels take their fill before scurrying away to hide surplus nuts from prying eyes. Bank and field voles carry off the acorns to their grass-lined nests, where they gnaw at the pointed end to reach the tasty kernel. Avaricious jays collect two or three acorns at a time, flying off

ABOVE Glorious autumn colour, displayed here by mature horse chestnut trees at Melplash Court.

RIGHT Jays habitually collect acorns throughout October from Dorset's oak trees. The birds eat some, but the majority are buried for a winter food supply, some of which become seedling oaks.

to bury them singly. Throughout winter many remain forgotten, but the new shoots of spring act as flags to mark where they are hidden. Both oak and animal benefit. Acorns are highly nutritious, whilst the tree depends on bird and animals to carry its seed away from the dark shade of its own canopy. In its lifetime of hundreds of years, only one acorn needs to grow into a tree for the oak to replenish itself.

October is the mating season for some of Dorset's deer. In the east of the county, a strange undulating whistle, not dissimilar to the sound of a squeaky gate, betrays the presence of a sika stag advertising it's rutting territory. Sika, or

ABOVE Sika deer are common in east Dorset. On Brownsea Island they have become used to humans and are relatively easy to observe.

RIGHT The low angle of the sun adds to the autumnal atmosphere in this quiet lane near Hilton.

Japanese deer were imported from the Far East during the nineteenth century for stocking deer parks. Escapes were inevitable, and feral herds are now common, particularly in east Dorset, where they can be seen late in the afternoon grazing on the lush marshes of Arne, or on Brownsea Island, where they are much less shy. In the woods of west Dorset and the Cranborne Chase, fallow bucks establish their rutting stands, vigorously defending their harems of does. The rut lasts for about a month and peaks around the third week of October. Throughout, mature bucks constantly issue their mating calls in a series of belching grunts. Established bucks

ABOVE In the distant autumn haze, the hills around Bridport
progressively fade into distinct layers, seen here from Lambert's
Castle with Hardy's Monument just visible on the skyline..

ABOVE The bar-tailed godwits at Ferrybridge probe the sand with their long bills in search of worms and molluscs.

see off younger amorous males, and in the frequent fights which ensue much damage can be done. At the end of the rut, the bucks are exhausted, and some of them simply wander off to die.

As the tide ebbs at Ferrybridge, at the Portland end of the Fleet, the exposed wet sand is dotted with the tiny hillocks of lugworm casts. Small parties of bar-tailed godwit work their way along the water's edge, probing the wet sand with their long bills. Occasionally a bird walks around its sunken bill, driving it downwards to capture a worm or mollusc.

The ringed plover is a permanent resident here. From a distance, it appears to be on wheels as it runs across the sand to grab stranded molluscs. The unusual ringed markings of this small wader enable it to blend perfectly with the pebbles of Chesil Beach, where it nests in summer.

ABOVE The ringed plover is resident in Dorset throughout the year. Like the bar-tailed godwit on the previous page, It can be seen on the mudflats at Ferrybridge at low tide.

LEFT During October, redwings arrive in Dorset to feed on holly berries. Later they will spend their days scavenging amongst leaf litter in woodland habitats.

Most of the summer birds have now left the county. By the end of the month different bird sounds echo in the valleys as waves of redwings arrive, uttering their wispy contact notes. Redwings do not breed in Dorset, but arrive here from Scandinavia to spend the winter. They feast on holly berries, systematically stripping one tree before starting on the next. Redwings are opportunists, taking advantage of whatever food is available at any given time. Only when winter finally arrives will they be forced to rummage through decomposing leaf litter in search of hibernating insects and grubs.

NOVEMBER

NOVEMBER

Smoke rising lazily from village chimney pots; the aroma of fermenting fruit; and the crackle and fizz of bonfire night mark the end of autumn. The most dramatic changes in the countryside are triggered as November dawns with autumn colours at their zenith, but wanes into the dismal beginnings of winter. Wild calls resonate in the hedgerows and in thickets, as birds flock together to feed on the abandoned last remnants of summer.

Just before dusk, cackling flocks of fieldfare drift high overhead. The fieldfare is a large thrush that migrates to Britain in the autumn. In mild weather, they feed in the open countryside on earthworms, much like blackbirds. They also

PREVIOUS PAGE Lush green herb Robert leaves, contrast with the discarded scarlet foliage of an acer tree.

ABOVE After leaf fall, the litter is broken down by bacteria and the nutrients are returned to the soil.

LEFT Flocks of fieldfares arrive in Dorset for the winter and visit orchards to feed on windfall apples.

ABOVE The silver birch (shown here at Hartland Moor) was the first tree to colonise Dorset after the last ice age. It is short lived but extremely hardy, and is especially abundant in the east of the county.

like fallen fruit, and can often be seen in orchards squabbling over the spoils of windfall apples.

On Dorset's heaths, the yellow leaves of silver birch trees provide a glittering contrast to the browning heather. The heaths appear barren and uninviting but are animated here and there by sprays of withering golden bracken. In the woods, the falling leaves reveal the stark skeleton of the trees. The vibrant colours of deciduous foliage is usually at its best during the first week of the month, but the autumn gales soon strip the branches and for a few days the ground is smothered with a colourful carpet of yellow, orange and red. Leaves rustle crisply underfoot, or are whipped up by the wind, finally becoming sodden by the rain. The process of decomposition begins as bacteria start to break down the nutrients, ultimately returning them to the earth. In deciduous woodland, everything is recycled naturally.

Animals and birds become increasingly busy as they prepare for winter. The summer moult now complete, new feathers and fur are worn to provide efficient insulation through the long winter nights. Hedgehogs and dormice feed voraciously to gain sufficient fat reserves to sustain them through the coming months of hibernation. A few days of mild weather at the start of the month can foster the illusion that autumn may linger. Brimstone butterflies and common darter dragonflies make their final sullies in the sunshine.

The rich flora of Dorset's lanes and coast is now reduced to seed heads and wilting stalks. Only a few flowers still produce a meagre show of feeble blooms in defiance of the changing seasons. The sprinkling of pink flowers on hedgebanks is the annual herb Robert. Lawn daisies struggle on to provide nectar for late flying bumblebees. In the east of the county, evening primrose displays its final blooms before the seeds ripen to offer winter fodder for finches. Translucent seedpods of honesty shimmer in the autumn sunlight and red rose hips and woody nightshade berries are exposed in the leafless hedges.

Along the coast, wildfowl have settled into their winter quarters. Like many species of wading bird, ducks and geese have moved south to Dorset, fleeing the harsh winters of their northern breeding grounds. Here they will stay to eke out a living until the beginning of spring and the instinct to breed calls them back to Scandinavia, Russia or the high Arctic. The numbers of Brent geese steadily increase in Poole Harbour and the Fleet as they fly in from their breeding grounds. Brent

ABOVE The lapwing has declined as a breeding species in Dorset. In early winter, flocks of these wading birds gather at Lodmoor to feed in the marshes.

BELOW The goldcrest is a permanent resident in Dorset, and its numbers are swollen in autumn by birds arriving from the north.

BELOW The first frosts of the year soften the hawthorn berries to make them palatable for winter thrushes.

ABOVE Hedgehogs increase their fat reserves by feeding eagerly throughout November before going into hibernation at the end of the month.

RIGHT On late autumn mornings, resting insects like this crane fly are often covered in water droplets from the overnight mist.

geese are completely adapted to marine life and can often be seen resting on the water, even during periods of extreme cold. They feed on eelgrass and seaweeds, which thrive in mud and sand at mid-tide level. These small, dark geese make an impressive aerial display as they commute between favoured roosting and feeding locations.

As nights continue to lengthen and temperatures steadily fall, the need for small birds to feed increases. Ripe seeds and fruits are plentiful in November, and wild berries are softened by the first frosts to make them more appetising. Thrushes and blackbirds begin to harvest crab apples and eat the rich red fruits of pyracantha and cotoneaster shrubs, while finches feed on burdock, teasel and nettle seeds.

ABOVE Seedheads of old man's beard decorate the crowns of every shrub on the hillside at Fontmell Down.

Once again, winter flocks begin to form as woodland birds join together to scavenge in bushes and along hedgerows. Parties of tits and finches descend on garden bird feeders. Man's generosity is not without risks. While flocking offers some advantages, it also invites danger. Regular congregations of small birds feeding together attract the attention of sparrowhawks. The sparrowhawk has always maintained a healthy population in Dorset, even during the 1960's when the use of pesticides led to a drastic decline of their numbers nationally. This woodland hawk thrives on a diet of living birds. Small birds like sparrows and tits are its most common victims, though it can easily kill a woodpigeon. The sparrowhawk is an opportunist predator, relying upon the element of surprise, together with speed to catch its daily quota of prey.

One bird at risk is the siskin, which arrives in Dorset during early November. These small yellow-green finches feed on alder seeds, and keep in contact with each other with twittering calls. Alder woodlands, such as at Higher Hyde Heath, support over-wintering flocks of siskins. Their other habitats include water meadows and riverbanks, where alder trees thrive in the damp ground.

As the first hints of winter become apparent, voles, woodmice and even insect-eating shrews seek refuge in human dwellings. At night they sneak into cottage and barn, where they can benefit from the warmth and dryness to remain active throughout winter.

If November is mild and damp, fungi will continue to produce fruiting bodies in woods and copses. Although fungi

ABOVE One of the birds at risk from the sparrowhawk is the siskin, which arrives in Dorset during November.

RIGHT Sparrowhawks pick off the weaker small birds, enabling stronger, fitter individuals to pass their genes on to future generations, which in turn benefits the prey species.

are present throughout the county, the greatest variety of these fascinating life forms occurs in deciduous woodland. Puddletown Forest boasts a wide range, including the yellow antler fungus, which emerges amongst the mosses on the woodland floor.

There is a certain melancholy about the look of the countryside after the leaves have fallen. By the end of the month the change of seasons is complete. Cooler conditions bring frost and fog at dawn, while trees stand naked and hedgerows are bare. The year in Dorset has entered its dotage as autumn finally succumbs to the advance of winter.

A brief moment of enchantment as early morning fog drifts across the fields near Beaminster in late November.

The bank vole is a common mammal occurring in copses and woodland throughout the county. It is vegetarian and feeds on fruit and green shoots.

DECEMBER

DECEMBER

Describing a Dorset winter in *Far From the Madding Crowd*, Thomas Hardy wrote of its arrival in stages, 'wherein might have been successively observed the retreat of the snakes, the transformation of the ferns, the filling of the pools, a rising of fogs, the embrowning of frost, the collapse of the fungi, and an obliteration by snow.'

Snow seems less frequent than when Hardy was writing, but little else has changed. December means diminishing daylight, raw shivery winds, sudden heavy rain beating down the withering vegetation. Ice crystals glint on the stately seed heads of hogweed, teasel and dock. Cobwebs thaw into sparkling prisms of water droplets in the low wintry sun. On the heaths, the white trunks of dormant birches stand stark and austere against the desolate background. We cheer ourselves with preparations for Christmas and the New Year, making December a month which can pass almost unnoticed in the countryside.

An overnight gale can strip deciduous trees of their last few leaves, making evergreen trees and shrubs suddenly more conspicuous. Holly and ivy bring a splash of life to the most dormant hedgerow. Ivy's colourful foliage has made it a symbol of friendship and longevity. Prior to Christian times it was believed that holly offered protection against evil forces, and sprays were brought indoors to ward off harmful spirits. Certainly the prickly leaves afford fine protection, and many creatures seek out this native evergreen for shelter and food.

Insects remain hidden beneath a blanket of leaf litter or in holes and crevices. Many pass the winter in egg form, some of them underwater in ponds and lakes. At times of intense cold,

PREVIOUS PAGE Snipe can be found in wet meadows and bogs, especially during cold winter weather. Their zigzag flight is an effective defence against falcons and other winged predators.

RIGHT The foliage of field rose, tinged with late autumn colour and edged with the ice crystals of a December frost.

ABOVE Sadly, the barn owl has declined to a point where it is quite a rarity throughout England. It still occurs in small breeding pockets in Dorset, along the coast and in farmland in the west of the county.

dragonfly nymphs and other aquatic larvae can be seen frozen in surface ice. On December nights, the winter moth (*Operophtera brumata*) flutters around lighted windows. Unlike the male, the small spider-like female is flightless, crawling up a tree to await the attentions of males, in this their mating season. Winter moth caterpillars hatch in spring, becoming serious pests of fruit trees.

On the coast, the beaches are abandoned, save for a few hardy dog walkers. Rock pipits and black redstarts flit amongst the seaweed near Lyme Regis, Charmouth and West Bay. The rock pipit is resident all year on the Dorset coast but the black redstart is a winter visitor occasionally seen feeding amongst the tousled ribbons of dried seaweed. The best thing about December in Dorset for those who love birds is the vast accumulation of waders and wildfowl that gather along the

ABOVE Clear, settled weather this month results in significant changes in temperature between day and night, which produces mist in the valleys. This picture of Gerrards Hill near Beaminster was taken early one December morning as mist circled the hill.

Dorset coast. Rafts of ducks crowd the sheltered waters of Radipole Lake, the Fleet lagoon and Poole Harbour. As well as tufted ducks, which are principally fresh water birds and seldom seen on dry land, there are teal, wigeon, shoveller and shelduck. The teal is a dabbling duck, happiest searching for aquatic midge larvae in the shallows. Wigeon are grazers and feed on various grasses on dry land but never venture far from water. The shoveller 'dabbles' on the water surface, sieving animal and plant matter over the fine, comb-like plates which line the edges of its bill. Despite its dark chestnut markings and white plumage, the shelduck seems uncertain as to whether it's a goose or a duck, waddling at low tide across the mudflats in search of crabs and shrimps like a goose, but upending itself like a duck when feeding beneath the water on vegetation.

Waders' calls echo across the water as tides fall and the birds start to move. Flocks of redshank, dunlin and ringed plover twist and turn with perfectly orchestrated movements. Turnstones forage amongst the pebbles in small flocks at

ABOVE The low-lying meadows around East Stoke flood during prolonged wet weather in winter.

RIGHT The clover-like leaves of wood sorrel can be seen throughout winter, nestled in crevices and hollows of mature deciduous trees.

Ferrybridge and Christchurch, and the haunting cries of curlew epitomise the wildness of the Dorset coast in winter. Oystercatchers form huge flocks, flashing their black and white wing markings when taking to the air. The quick erratic flight and rasping call of the snipe distinguishes it from other wading birds, especially in times of intense cold when it is forced to visit freshwater bogs and creeks.

Short eared owls also turn up along the coast, as well as on scrubby chalk downland. They hunt in daylight on winter afternoons, silently floating low over rough ground or gliding and wheeling in search of voles. In recent years, numbers of short eared owls over-wintering in Dorset have increased

significantly, especially on Portland and the landward side of the Fleet.

The barn owl was once common throughout Dorset, but the population of this ghostly, nocturnal hunter has declined to a point where it now occurs in only a few isolated pockets. Modern farming methods have been blamed - as has the increase in traffic, as they are apt to hunt along roadside verges. A few pairs of barn owls still breed in West Dorset, and December is a good month to see them, as they also hunt in daylight during winter. Typically, they flit between fence posts, silently watching for voles in ditches and rough pasture.

ABOVE An overnight snow fall transforms Hooke Park into a winter wonderland.

OPPOSITE PAGE TOP LEFT The greenshank is not a common wader, but Poole Harbour usually supports a small number of birds through the winter.

OPPOSITE PAGE LOWER LEFT Red breasted mergansers are sawbill ducks, so-called because of a series of sharp serrations along the edges of the bill which enable them to grip slippery fish.

OPPOSITE PAGE FAR RIGHT Long tailed tits work the hedgerows in small flocks, roosting huddled together in a tight ball.

rosettes of primrose leaves hold out the promise of spring. The blooms of winter heliotrope begin to show in damp hedge banks and the catkins of native trees start to expand. On the last night of the year the hoarse, rasping bark of a vixen echoes across the frosty fields. All else is silent until a clatter of church bells erupts to chime in the new. The year passes, gone forever to become nothing more than memories and experiences. But the cycle of life goes on as the changing seasons continue to flow and ebb. In the months ahead, another year will unfold and we will watch with wonder as the dramas of nature are again performed in Dorset's wild places.

LEFT Bare trees line a bend in the River Frome at Lower Bockhampton.

BELOW Ladybirds hibernate in clusters. They give off an unpleasant odour, which deters predators. The greater the number of insects the more effective the smell.

After dark you can sometimes hear the piercing hoarse screech that is their territorial cry.

Elsewhere inland, woodland birds feed continuously during the short days. Crossbills use their specialised beaks to extract seed from pinecones in the conifer plantations of Wareham Forest and blue tits dislodge ash keys as they search for hidden insects. Typically in December, many of us put out food on bird tables. Once started, it is essential to keep on doing so until early spring, as small birds become reliant upon regular food. If the supply ceases, valuable energy is expended searching elsewhere, which can tip the balance between survival and death.

Not all garden birds readily visit bird tables and feeders, and most species that do have discovered them by accident. Long-tailed tits were almost unknown as bird table visitors in Dorset until the late 1980's, but now they are one of the commonest birds to be seen. They have recently been joined by the goldfinch, now frequently spotted hanging on peanut baskets. Other birds that are beginning to overcome their shyness and visit Dorset gardens include the nuthatch and all three of the woodpeckers.

Even as we all gather for carol services or hurry around doing the last of our Christmas shopping, signs of new life are already stirring. Spikes of daffodil foliage thrust up through the leaf mould and snowdrop buds thicken and split. The first

ABOVE The weasel has a long thin body to accommodate its
organs and to enable it to follow its prey of mice and voles into
their narrow runs and homes.

Looking out over the Fleet lagoon and Chesil Beach towards the
open sea. The sun rises and falls in the sea at this time of year,
often producing dramatic skies reflected in the water at either end
of the day.

INDEX

Page numbers in **bold** refer to illustrations